the left hand of god

a soul's love poems

john p. davidson

HeartWorks
PUBLISHING

HeartWorks Publishing is a trademark of HeartWorks Publishing Company
Cover Photo: John P. Davidson (Copyright 2014 John P. Davidson)
Cover design: Charlotte Hollis and John P. Davidson
Interior Book Design: Booknook.biz
Sorts Mill Goudy font: theleagueofmoveabletype.com

Davidson, John P. (John Philip), 1947.

     The left hand of God: a soul's love poems / John P.
     Davidson.
        pages cm
     LCCN 2014904669
     ISBN 978-0-9882557-3-9
     Poems.

     I. Title.

     PS3604.A9468L68 2014   811'.6
     QBI14-600043

ISBN: 978-0-9882557-3-9

Library of Congress Control Number: 2014904669

About the Cover Photo: This beautiful object is from the author's collection and is of unknown origin. It appears to be an African baby carrier.

HeartWorks Publishing Company
P.O. Box 6
Raton, New Mexico 87740
USA
www.heartworkspublishing.com

OTHER BOOKS BY
JOHN P. DAVIDSON

The Soul's Critical Path: Waking Down to the Soul's Purpose, the
Body's Power, and the Heart's Passion

Soul Tribes and Tambos: Communities for Souls on the Move

For Darlene and my first soul mate, Janie

The wave is not the water.
The water merely told us
about the wave moving by.

R. Buckminster Fuller (1895-1983)

TABLE OF CONTENTS

PART ONE

LOVE POEMS

PART TWO

THE LEFT HAND OF GOD

PART ONE

LOVE POEMS

LOVE SURPRISES JUST LIKE THAT

The hunters race
to that place
the shaman has seen
in her dream
and wait watching,
watching for the game to come,
but behind the hunters
the quarry comes
silent and soft,
stalking the hunters,
giving itself
to their spears.
Love surprises
just like that.

Between heaven and earth
my soul forms up
and trembles unseen
like night's dew
held upon spider's web
stretched ever so delicately
from here to there
until Sun rises
and explodes my soul
into rainbow light.
Love surprises
just like that.

In my dream Kali came
dark, luminous and large,
smiling and laughing,
kissing me,
taking me upon her chest
before pulling a gun
from between our hearts,

sweetly offering
who I thought I was
complete annihilation.
Love surprises
just like that.

I sat quietly this morning
slipping past fear's cold bars
while blissful tears
poured out,
blessing my cheeks
and heart.
Love surprises
just like that.

And you have come
to me
ever so quietly,
your heart stalking mine
from behind.
It doesn't matter
what I think I know.
Heart lives
where the mind can't go.
Love surprises
just like that.

SOUL MATES

Soul mates
arrive like treasures lost
and found again,
joy resurrected
from ancient grave,
daffodils shining
through winter's shroud
and clouds racing from
Sun's warm face.

There is great gift in the mystery
that is foretold
in Love's absence
from our eyes.
What scheme is written
beneath this happy reprise?
What surprise lies
beyond our meeting again
in the forgotten purpose
of meeting before?

That is not for humans to know
until the play is played
and the script unscrolled
and only then
if we catch the drift.
The author's irony,
the player's paradox.
Fate takes the lead
while destiny lurks.
Attend now the play.
Let the drama unfold
in soul rhythm and rhyme,
not in mind's future time.

Remember just this,
my beloved mate.
There is no gold
nor magic
in scrying our fate.
Souls wrote the play
for their edification
not we for ours.
We must act the part
and feel our way
by the way we feel
and that way know
the play by heart.

WERE YOU THERE?

Were you there?
Souls will ask
when old ones gather
below heaven's hill.
Were you there
when Money failed
and Nature wailed
while Kali reigned
and Chaos feigned destruction?

The coming storm
long foreseen on Heaven's screen
has souls scrambling
to enlist again
as dimensions thin,
when only absolute attention
and heart and breath
will find the path.

These volunteers race
to the place
where things are happening
with such complete possibility,
so pregnant with Creation,
that they may lose themselves in fear
or mere compassion for birth's pain
and must remember once again
the cosmic question.

The old warriors are back
heating up Earth's fire
amidst the storm,
laying their swords in,
tempering their steel
to steal upon Fear,

to give proof to the One Truth
that no thing is more important
than being and receiving Love.

Were you there?
Souls will ask
when old ones gather
below Heaven's hill.
Were you there,
were you present,
and did you love
with all your breath
and all your heart?

WHERE ARE THE OLD ONES?

Where are the *chakaruna,*
the old ones
who know,
who know who they are
and why we are here?
Where are they,
the ones who bridge,
who bridge heaven to earth,
whose hearts
center the universe?

Don't look on the mountain,
in the forest
or the jungle,
across the great river
or behind ashram walls.
The forests are floating
in the rivers,
the mountains mined,
our hearts escaping
only by benign neglect.

The old ones are back
disguised in young faces,
fresh from heaven
with tablets glowing
in their hands.
They are awakening
to who they are,
still shaking off
fate's enforced forgetting
felt like jet lag
multiplied by millennia,
their commandments writ large
on souls still smoking,

their eyes burning
with heaven's fire
and coffee.

They are in the airports
moving fast and wide,
feeling the planet,
taking stock,
triaging the carnage,
trying to remember
who they *really* are,
what their work is *this* time
while things heat up
and humanity teeters.

I say
walk with them,
wake them quickly,
tell them the one thing
they need to know.
I say
show them *how* to know,
how to listen with their *hearts*
so they will know again
who they are,
why we are here
and what they have to do.

SOUL REUNION

Do souls kiss before they part?

I remember so
It could not be otherwise
than my soul kissing yours
and promising
the most delicate
of promises
to meet again,
to come finally
to this place
where stand you with me
and I with you.
And did your soul kiss mine?
I remember so
and yearn for the telling
of your memory of it
and the promise made you me.

Awakening now
in journey's midst,
my memory arises,
written on heart's cavewall
long abandoned
by fate's forced forgetting.
I remember now.
My tears mark that kiss
with welcome
as we are welcomed
by those who remained home
and know you now
because they
as I
knew you then.

How lost I this
and you
to wander so long
and across so far?
How lost I me
and remember not
from where I came
but recognize myself in you?
How delicate
to find you now
in this singular moment,
this tiny intersection
of luminous threads
in the vast fabric of time.
How precious
to find you now
at this crossing
of disparate paths
that could have twisted
another way.
What mystery
they did not so twist away,
that our eyes were met here
not turned,
that you recovered your memory
in my voice.

There is no answer
to disturb my wonder.

Only know
how precious this promise
that binds us together,
that holds hearts together,
that gathers together
our souls
face to face
from the mystery
of disparate journeys.

What aching longing
becomes this infinite sweetness,
this kiss
of soul reunion.

CHOKE ON LOVE

Just as I'm falling
in the Love
with you
voices crowd round
crying and wailing.
Stop!
they say.
*How can you stand
the heartbreak
once more?*
as if their concern
were about me.
And what of their hearts?
Don't be a fool!

And all the while
I race to the Love
and to you.
My fear is greater by far
than theirs,
they braver than I
to stand back
from the Love,
to embrace cold fear.
Such courage have they.
No!
I say to them.
*My insanity I choose
over your sanity.*

I can't hear them now,
those settlers,
those squatters
who stay put
clinging to small plots.
Give me vastness.

What else is there
but Love?
What risk
can the Love bring
that is not multiplied
by not loving?

Small love's pain
has been so sweet,
can I bear
great Love's joy?
I'll risk dissolving
in *that* Love.
I'll risk flying dangerously
into your arms
before dying safely
in my own.
I'll ride the wind horse bareback
in moonless dark
and unknowable night
before denying this Love.

So I race home to the Love
where stand you also.
I say
Let me choke on Love
than safely starve.

LET HER BREATHE

These hot tears
hold my apology to you,
woman.
They burn my lips
like the ancient memory
of your blood
on my hands
is burned in my soul.

This tearful choking
is your last breath
swallowed into me
carried by earth
a hundred generations
to speak now
from the cells
of this body.

Men, all men,
carry this memory,
are capable of this horror,
are responsible
to root this out,
to say
not again,
not in this body.

The she in me
has also suffered long
beneath the patriarchal mind
of the weak he in me.
She has suffered long
waiting to be seen,
praying to survive,
praying to be heard.

To my brothers
I say
Now is the time.
The earth will not wait.
Women cannot wait.
Go deep.
Remember.
Help her rise.
Let her breathe.

HOW DOES LOVE COME?

How does love come?

Like wind blowing
through the cracks
of some old house
where homeless huddle,
billowing up
their small fire
until flames consume
the house?
It comes like that,
pushing past cold fear.

Like the room empties
when I've said my dream
and sung my song
but for you
still standing there?
It comes like that,
smiling into
soul's bright eyes.

Like earth tremors
beneath my feet
shifting the ground
as I balance
in some new way
releasing fear
into soft sobbing?
It comes like that,
teaching my body
soul rhythms,
teaching my soul
earth songs.

Like this morning's dream
where I leaned forward
and touched the neck
of the black stallion
from astride his back
and felt the strong muscles
wet and warm
and saw his wild eye
and whispered clicking sounds
telling him to go
where he will?
It comes like that,
powering freedom
in swift strong strides.

And your love,
through your love,
Love comes
and holds me
in your arms
and rocks me
whispering my name
softing, softing, softing.
It comes like that,
touching my soul to the body
and my body
to the earth

Yes,
and not like that at all.
I can't say
how Love comes.
It just comes and comes.

STRING THEORY

Fear and pain
are no more than God's ways
of nudging the sleeping soul,
tugging at your heart strings,
tightening and tuning,
getting you ready
for the concert,
inviting you
to wake up
and
play your heart song.
Your Audience is waiting.

TASTING DEATH

Sink down now,
she whispered,
beneath the shimmering surface.
Go all the way down.
Do not drink or drown.
Do not linger.
Remember who you are.
One taste is enough.
Hurry back.
No time to waste.
Create Love's story.
Only heart completes.

What blessing
to taste this furtive kiss
from that strange beauty
who appears laughing
and turns away,
beckoning me to follow,
leaving me breathless
with heart pounding
and passion waking wild.
What else to do but follow?

What blessing
to sample Death's precious gift
that restores to soul
a memory of home.
It is not a book to read
nor story written
but memory recovered
of purpose lost
and agreements forgotten
amidst fate's painful journey.

What blessing
to sneak beneath the tent
at this tendered age
and spy the circus,
all doubt erased.
The taste is in my mouth.
I have soul eyes now
and heaven's music in my ears.
What else to do
but play the clown
and travel with tigers?

INNER MARRIAGE

Before she came
you dreamed her.
Awaken fully now.
Soul's mate cannot wait
Fate's further twist and turn.
She is your beloved
and your betrothed.
Soul's *be love*
and *be truth*
speak through her.
Mount the wind horse
and grasp his mane.
Heart-whisper the body's name.
Race to her
and dance the night.
Lift up the sun
with lover's laughter
and rainbowed eyes.
Let nothing stand between.
What can keep you apart now?

SOME SOULS SURPRISE

Some souls surprise
our hearts
with bodies younger
than their eyes
and knowing quite beyond
this Earth reprise.

It is beyond
my knowing
how Fate contrives
our deeper lessons,
dressing our teachers
in such disguise.

No surmise whispers
their coming.
The Beloved so delights
in playful unpredictability
as I delight
in the paradox of you.

EARTH LOVES HER HOT SUN

This morning
I came to you
not gently,
not like windless ripples
lapping the shore,
not like moon shadows
lying softly
upon bed clothes,
not like soft sunlight
waking the day.

No.
I came to you
full on
without warning,
my hot breath
and insistent hands
like wind raging
across open plains,
flattening grass
in its path,
pushing you down
beneath raw yearning
and the heat of high noon.

Oh.
Earth loves her hot sun
and wild winds
that sweep sleep
from her eyes
while she murmurs
sweet laughter
beneath it all,
containing it all,

and I laugh at this play
knowing well
how you love
this tickling tongue.

And then we rest
remembering,
remembering how long
the soul must hold the body
before she feels safe
and loved,
how much the body must heal
before it can open,
before it can invite the soul in,
all the way in,
how long the courtship
of body by soul
before Heaven can touch Earth
through your body and mine.

Earth loves her hot sun
because you
with your long
and steadfast work,
have connected
what Earth and Sun
cannot,
and my love for you
spreads wide and far
like hot sun shining
on the breast of Earth.

SOUL YEARNING

I yearn most for the yearning,
to rise awake on its wave
and ride its flood,
to freefall from its heights
to depths carved by cataract force,
then to drift gently in its silken flow
before standing in the shallows,
face to the sun
arms outstretched
body bloodied and brilliant
daystars dancing about my feet
resting only to take another breath
before diving again and again
in one continuous motion
of gratitude and joy.

No resting place can satisfy
that whose only way is to move,
no object large enough to dam it.
It feels so good just to feel.
So I yearn for the yearning
and surrender to the deepest current
where only absolute attention navigates,
where only absolute silence sings.

FORGET KISSING

Forget kissing
and demure looks.
Forget candled romance
and kindled poetry.
Forget flowers
and music,
even bodies sweltering
in sublime ecstasy.

What seduces my soul
is your truth
honestly spoken.
I cannot resist
the invitation
of lips parting
wet with words
of who you are.
My lips race
to respond,
offering up
my truth to you.

What penetrates more deeply
than truth
or receives more fully
than the yearning for it?
More love there is
in being
who we are.
More love is felt
in seeing
and being seen
face to face
soul to soul

and heart to heart
than mere naked bodies
can know.

What can follow such as this?
Well . . .
remember kissing?

NOT ANOTHER BORED GAME

Here's the game,
he said.

Another boring game?
she said.

Just the opposite.
he said.
Full attention required.
Tell me a secret,
something you've never
ever told anyone.
Say it as clear and strong
as you can.
Play that card here,
in the center
of my heart.
No discarding.
You have to play
all your secrets in time.
Start with one,
just a small one
if you like.

And if I do?
she said.
What next?

Your secret becomes
my hold card
he said.
I have to hold it
in my heart
and protect it
from all aggressors.

Like who?
Give me an example,
she said.

You know,
he said,
like judgment,
a very aggressive sin indeed.

And if you can . . .
she said,
I mean,
what if you can
really hold my secret?

Then we celebrate,
he said.
Every secret told
and heart-held
is a winner,
so we sing and dance
to welcome home
this tiny soul part
back from the shadow
where it hid.

Bring wine
if you like.
It may take a while.
We'll hold that truth
until it can't imagine
being anywhere else
but home
here
in our hearts.

And then?
she said.

Then it's my turn
he said.

How long does this game last?
she said.

As long as truth
remains unsaid,
he said.
And new truths awaken
within our souls each day.

Could take a lifetime.
Want to play?

DO WE THROW OURSELVES FROM HEAVEN?

Do we throw ourselves
from heaven?
I feel just that,
free falling,
flailing at dark air,
terrified of the ground
for which I yearn.

I must have forgotten
choosing this before.
The feeling is so familiar,
yearning to stay,
knowing the sweet comfort
and choosing against it,
yearning to go,
yearning for the work
that wants to be done.

I can hear heart's crust
breaking open,
crackling red hot,
racing into blue atmosphere,
racing toward Mother,
aiming for her dark ocean,
looking for dolphins
to take me to the shore
of my being
where I will stand
to dance
my dance.

MELTING

On clear winter days
I've snuggled naked
into the warming earth
among remnants
of melting snow.

I imagine this embrace
to be of the One
for whom I yearn,
The Beloved
in lovely She-guise.

I pray that she will
melt me too,
that she will
release the freezing grasp
of evolution's long dark winter,
that she will
thaw my crystalline waters,
that she will
emerge through my heart
singing songs of spring.

WHAT I CAN GIVE YOU?

Wondering
what it is
I could possibly
give to you,
I muse
and feel deeply
your gifts to me.

Your hand touching me
seems the hand of God
touching in me
what I cannot,
connecting me to
that in me
that loves
touch so much.

Your eye seeing me
seems the eye of God
seeing in me
what I cannot,
illuminating me
deep within
my own skin.

To know myself
in the mirror
of your clear eyes,
to feel myself thus,
I need not wonder more
what gift I can give to you.

DANGEROUS LOVE

The fantasy of love
felt far safer
than Love's reality.
Dangerous love
pushes up my spine
like a red-hot rod
setting fire to projections,
chasing out old fear
that conjured up
safe dolls in doll houses.

Dangerous love fills me
with frenzy
lifting me up
into blessed confusion.
The old being is fleeing.
The dam is breached.
Heart is set loose,
overflowing mountains.
What else to do
but learn to breathe
and swim deep waters?
Love's fierce grace
is in your face
and my eyes
caught in yours.

GREEN EYED LOVER

My Lover's kiss
is more magic
than any man's
imaginating,
Her sorcery
Source itself.
My eyes trance planted
with her green eyes
peel away layer
upon layer
of luminescent
serpentine garment
until reality is naked
and my head lies
upon angel breasts
of pure light.
She whispers
Let me take care of you
and the cosmos becomes my home
as soul enters the body
trance fixed
by her healing gaze.
Her sensuous embrace
trance sending
all my sense
into sinuous dance
ignites my shadow
into golden-blue fire,
trance fusing my spine
into light so intense
that every cell
is trance formed
as I awaken to the vibration of Her voice
and the embrace of Her arms.

I am be-earthed anew
born again
into bright moment
after bright moment
as She breathes into me
a sighing ecstasy
and pushes Her body
tingling into mine
making my back to arch
with all the strength
of the jungle cat
that claws flaws
from out my sight.

Come play,
she whispers
into mine ear,
trance muting it
to the sound of all
but her voice.
Dance barefooted
and barehearted
upon enlightened earth
and in dark forest.
Make your soul's desire
your sole desire.

What soul could resist
such seduction,
this sedition of senses
into soul service?
Not mine,
I sigh,
and raise my lips
for one more elucidating kiss.

I DIDN'T SEE IT COMING

I didn't see it coming,
your stepping up
and seeing inside
all at once,
except for some dark corners
that even I don't see.
I didn't try to hide.
Seldom do.
No one ever sees
really sees
or so I thought,
and I
standing there
saw your eyes
going right to my heart,
feeling like a man shot through,
staring at the hole,
wondering what happened
just before he falls.

And there you are
laughing,
smiling at the surprise
of seeing inside
like finding lovers naked
in the forest
where least you expect them,
and me
smiling at the surprise
and seeing inside too,
getting that you are wide open,
maybe a few dark corners,
but really really open
like you hadn't bothered
to comb your hair

because you just don't care
what people think.

And there we are
looking at each other
and just a bit past
to see if anyone else
spotted this hitch in time,
this growing glow,
letting the smiles ease back and big
until laughter creeps up again
and splits those smiles apart.

That's how I caught Love's scent
then Love's sight,
light pouring in
and bright.
Who before
no one could see,
I saw you,
and you saw me.

LOVE'S DEEPER LESSONS

What are you afraid of?
She whispered so softly
that the question was
no more than
compassionate heart opening,
no less than
the hand of God unfolding
like Lila's lilting laughter.

Just this,
he said.
There were women before you,
soul mates all,
whose deep love
denied me love,
who forced me
to love myself
teachers so rigorous
and perfect
it feels I have
only just survived,
only just awakened
to who they are,
to profound gratitude
for their meeting me here.
And you,
you have arrived so quickly
that my breath is taken away
like death's surprise.

Saying this he knew
the blessing of all that went before
placing him at your door
without old masks
without love hidden
from himself.

Saying this he knew
you were here to teach him also.
But teach him what?

I say to teach me
the taste of love unmasked
the dance of love embodied
to see love shining
to hear love's laughter
and feel love's screaming joy.
I say I will teach you the same.
And if I err in this judgment
(that is my fear)
what matters it at all
that I fall into love's deeper lessons?

All this he said
laughing at himself,
laughing at the irony
of interrupting flight
to talk of the wisdom
of having soared
into heart's rare air.

TO THE WOMAN
IN THE WHOLE FOODS MARKET

Some poems
are never written,
disappearing just beyond
a whisper.
Saying *Say that again?*
just doesn't cut it with poems.
They're on the move
like a cloud
that's a rabbit
then nothing at all.

It's not easy
being a poem,
hanging there
in the air
swirling waves
into word particles
like an angel trying to tickle us awake
with the tip of her wing feather
while we just scratch.

I've not noticed
more than one door
that opened
while I whistled by.
It's no little death
a poem not heard
and never said.
I feel like a murderer.
Not pathological
mind you.
Just negligent poemicide.

Like that beautiful woman
in the Whole Foods Market.
I saw her in produce
twice
then passed her cart again
in soups
where she smiled
as our eyes met,
then again in cheeses
and the salad bar.
She showed up again
across from my table
with her lunch
a book
and another smile.
What does a woman have to do?

I was just too much in my head
to feel that she was feeling
what I was feeling.
What lay behind her door?
Well. . .
regrets only
if the poet isn't going to show.

That was a door opened,
a meeting missed,
a poem killed
before its prime,
sweetness whispering
loud enough to hear
without any ear at all
if I were not so shy,
too distracted by some bullshit protocol
to hear that poem
and say those words out loud.
Poems don't care about protocol,
nor do some women,
I imagine.

Did I say
by the way
that a poem
is like a woman?
Just listen
and watch what emerges.
Pay attention
I remind myself.
Everything we need
is right here.
Always.
Love is no more
than listening
with everything we are
and celebrating what sings out.
We bring being into being
by seeing.
Give those visions voice.
Now.

Note to Whole Foods:
Would you be kind enough to post this?
She was the blonde one
with snow boots
and snow pants
unzipped in the back
up to the knee
and a vee-neck
with a silver pendant necklace.
Did I say she had a very nice smile?
And a gallon of milk.

JUST FRIENDS

Can a man
just be friends
with a woman?
Just friends
as they say?

Let me start
with that *just* part.
Huge word
this word just
that we use
just to say
something less
about so much more,
to diminish what follows,
to imply friends
are less than lovers
without saying it
outright.

I'll say it.
There's lesser love
between lovers
whose friendship is foreplay
than between just-friends
whose honesty penetrates as deeply as lovers do,
whose intimacy embraces more warmly
than mere lovers parting.

It's as though *girlfriend*
means less friend than girl,
as though we've forgotten
that girlfriend
was two words
before it was one,
as though friendship

with a girl
is an *as though* friendship,
as though we are friends,
but not really.
Maybe it's just
a personal confession.
Well . . . not *just.*
Let us not
diminish confession either.

And doesn't calling her the *girl*
diminish the woman?
I would a woman
not a girl
meet me there
honest
intimate
eye to eye
naked
with her clothes on
and the man in me
meet her
just there
not as just friends,
no,
but for friendship
not foreplay
but for play
just play.
Wait,
no,
not just play . . .
just . . .
play.
Let us not diminish
love nor play
and come to neither.

But that's just
what I say.
What does the Beloved say?
I heard just this:
Love each and all the same
and you will find the one
you love the more.

WINTER TALES

Sun and Moon bed
behind cloudy veil
while Wind curls
around its tail
and sparkling flakes
come to rest
softing, softing
on Mother's breast.

Fall seasons us
just so
that Winter's tender arms
around us go
and invite that
we go slow
and curl about
our tales.

LISTEN CAREFULLY NOW

Listen carefully now,
her lover whispered.
Do not mistake
what we are doing
for mere bodies making love.

There is so much more
that goes on here.
Bodies become bored.
What excited them
just moments ago
simply tires now.
The banquet loses its appeal
and we push back from the table
wondering why we ate so much.

You needn't wonder,
he whispered.
Just remember
who you are
and why we are here.

I know your story,
he whispered.
I've heard it many times,
a woman crying her pain,
trying to make a home
in a burned out building,
trying to find herself
amidst shuttered and shattered men,
hiding the body
that is all others see of her.
But you came
to use this body.
Its pain shouts out
with purpose.

It would awaken your sleeping soul
from this dark dream.

What good is some soul
that forgot why it came?
What good a soul
that doesn't enlist the body
to its cause?
The soul is not some tourist
touching down for the day
and leaving before dark
with trinkets.
No.
Alchemists are we.
Let us conjure the soul
from its sleepy place
and mix it with time.
Let soul seduce body
with cosmic Love
and stir electric mysteries of heaven
into magnetic elements of earth.

I know what I'm about
when we get naked,
he whispered.
I intend my touch
to tune your body
to ecstatic song
that awakens the soul
from slumber.
My desire will conspire
with yours,
wasting no more time,
going right for the God spot,
bringing your body
to heights and depths
that will awake that sleeping soul.
And you can do the same
for me.

The sun has lain
on the water
all these days,
he whispered.
The air is warm and sultry.
The mud is cool
and sinuous around my feet.
Come my love.
Let the soul remember
who it is
and why it came.
Breathe the body
until it invites
the awakened soul back in.
And do not mistake
what we are doing
for mere bodies making love.

BEAUTY TURNS MY HEAD

Beauty turns my head.
The soul moves
like metal to a magnet.
Mountains and waters,
brilliant skies,
bright sun,
dark forests
and city lights alike,
like every soul I meet—
all draw the soul close
into Love's warm embrace.

No wonder I forgot
that other beauty,
my home before this home.
No wonder dying is so hard.
This beauty turns our heads
and holds our eyes.
We forget who we are
and where we came from.
Even souls get lost,
some in beauty,
some in the body's pain.

Turn your head now,
dear friend.
There is infinite beauty
where you came from.
Turn your head
and head home.
Let Love's light catch your eye.
Trade this beauty for *that* beauty.
The gifts you brought
have all been delivered.
Nothing more to do.

Dying is no more
than turning around,
going out the door you entered
what seems only minutes ago.
Your old body is tired
and will drop soon.
Turn your head,
dear friend,
turn your head.
Awe—Love's sweetest alias—
will light your way.

PART TWO

THE LEFT HAND OF GOD

THE LEFT HAND OF GOD

Who can understand what God is?
I know I can't.
But I know something's behind all this.
I can feel it.
This planet didn't just happen.
Look at this body.
Can you make one?
Can you make water?
Or a galaxy?
Can you create life?
I didn't think so.
All the scientists put together can't.
How does breath come?
They don't even know that.
God is just a name
for something we don't understand.
Not a man.
Not a woman.
Something we don't understand.
But something *is*.
So I'll say that God *is*.
Let's start there.

Even God had to start somewhere.
So God made something new.
Some say it was light.
Some say it was sound.
But I say God started with here and there.
Light has to start somewhere.
Even light goes from here to there.
Just like sound.
I say God made point A and point B.
And put a line in between.
That's a big hint to who you are.

Two parts that are connected.
Parts that can't exist without the other.
I'll call that *polarity*.
Everything God made has two parts.
Was there another way to do it?
Maybe, but that's the way God did it.
There were lots of steps that followed.
I think God had humans in mind.
For a very particular purpose.
But that gets ahead of the story.

As I said, God made light and sound.
Scientists made up new names for those two.
Photons and wave/particles.
Both have frequency.
Frequency is a going forth
and a coming back.
A conversation.
A relationship.
Something that connects
here to there.
Polarity, like I said.
From light and sound, God made atoms.
Atoms have a here and a there too.
Parts held together by this polarity.
That really got things started.
God herded atoms into molecules.
Molecules have polarity too.
Molecules formed cells.
Scientists first thought cells had walls.
But they figured it out.
Cells are held together by . . .
po-lar-ity.

Well, rocks are made of molecules.
God tweaked those molecules
into something that could grow.
We've called those plants.
God tweaked some more.

Molecules that could move around.
Let's call those animals.
God was obviously heading somewhere.
God tweaked again.
Molecules that grow and move and choose.
Let's call those humans.
Humans have something
nothing else on the planet has.
That would be freedom.
You are that freedom.
Even if you haven't noticed yet.
What can you do with freedom
and all those molecules?
Maybe that's what God is curious about.
Maybe *you* embody God's curiosity.
But I'm ahead of the story again.

So, a lot has been happening,
and it's taken a long time.
Scientists call it evolution.
Some think we need to understand
where we've been.
Then maybe we'll understand
where we're going.
I have a little different idea about that.
I think if we understand where we're going,
then we might understand where we've been.
And maybe we can meet in-between those ideas.
Polarity, yes?

Some people, bless their hearts,
think with their brains.
Brains are a good and beautiful thing.
For sure.
God intended that we use them.
Other people think with their hearts.
We call it imagination.
And some of us think with both.
Brains and hearts are very different.

Which is why God gave humans both.
Humans would need to know where to go.
And how to get there.
Two different things,
if you think about it.
Hearts know where we need to go next.
Nobody says "follow your head."
People who know anything
know to follow their hearts.
And once you know where to go,
head can make the reservations.
Two beautiful kinds of intelligence.
Linked together.
Hmmm… polarity again.

By the way, who listens to the head?
And who feels into the heart?
Don't worry if you're talking to yourself.
It's a good thing.
You're the most important person
to talk to.
There's a hint about who you are.
It's that polarity again.

So, if everything is a polarity,
humans must be two things.
I'll just spit this out.
God made souls, and God made bodies,
and humans are the combination of both.
Now, which one of those are you?
Let me tell you,
that is the biggest question
humans have to answer.

Well, it's no mystery
humans are confused about that.
Otherwise, we wouldn't be in this mess.
God knows how valuable a little ignorance is.
God knew that creation is hard work.

Souls would have to do some learning first.
Before we can do the hard part,
we have to prepare.
God only knows,
no one has done this before.
So souls have to start young and grow up.
Just like the bodies they landed in.
Souls have to learn how to use those bodies.
And the body's senses and feelings and brains.

Look at this from God's point of view.
God had to get the planet ready.
Humans are so delicate.
Too hot or too cold won't work.
It took a long time.
Using tiny vibrations
gathering molecules into forms,
what with those molecules
taking their own sweet time.
I can just hear some angel saying that
in low, resonant tones.
IT TOOK LONGER
THAN SIX OF YOUR EARTH DAYS.
It took a lot longer than six days.
There had to be water,
and a way for it to clean itself.
The soil had to be good enough to grow food,
and have a way to restore itself.
There needed to be animals.
Animals for food and to help with the work.
Even animals that could hold our hearts.
Because our hearts have a heavy load to carry.
And plants for food, medicine, and making things.
And plants like vines and cactus and mushrooms.
Because humans need help to see.
But I'll get to that later.

And there was a very special thing God did.
When you stand around in nature,

you feel better.
I know you know about this.
Right on the surface of the earth,
where we live,
there is a frequency.
That polarity again.
The very same frequency
as your nervous system
when it is relaxed.
Alpha.
7.83 Hz.
Strong enough to bring your nervous system
right along with it.
And we've done our best to screw that up.
With even stronger electromagnetic waves
that run right over that frequency.
With cell phones and cell towers,
and with power lines and electric grids.
And chemicals that poison
the frequencies of healthy cells.
While doctors scratch their heads
and dispense more chemicals.
Wonder why more of us are getting sick?
That's no big mystery.

But back to the story.
Arranging earth took a long time to do.
God used light and sound,
herding those molecules into shape.
There is a good God reason for that.
With light and sound,
God could keep updating the software
that runs on that molecular hardware.
Think about it.
You and I get information downloads all the time.
We don't know where it comes from.
Do you feel like me?
I don't know where ideas come from.
Neither does any scientist.

They may not be mine at all.
Maybe I just get in the way
of some wave/particle God sent.
At least that's what I try to do.
Maybe that's how creation goes forward.
Learning from experience,
and learning by listening.
Souls might just be the software manager
for those earth bodies.
Listening is how we update
from time to time
to see if the prime software designer
has something new.
Hmmm... Heaven and earth.
Polarity again.

Just think of all the things NASA had to do,
getting an astronaut on the moon.
I think souls may be a lot like those astronauts.
Can you imagine a soul, like a tiny drop of God?
Imagine it exploding out of heaven in a blast of light!
Can you see a soul heading toward this tiny body?
Just like a raindrop plummets down
and hits a drop of earth.
Like I said, polarity.

Well, those souls landed in the middle of the body.
And woke up with a little memory problem.
Souls do tend to sleep on the way.
Just like astronauts going way out there
would have to sleep on the way.
Just imagine if you were a soul
and woke up in a strange body.
Like that astronaut,
you have to start from scratch.
You put on your earth suit.
And figure out how it works.
I can just hear the questions.
Like, what do you do with these things,

these hands and legs?
What about these feelings?
Oooooh! I like that person,
the warm one with the food!
And these sounds and smells.
And this mind, oh boy!
What a trip!
All of this is new to a soul.
It doesn't have any parts of its own.
No feelings or senses of its own.
No brain to process thoughts with.
This soul just borrows this body.
It needs to learn how to use it pretty fast
if it's going to get some work done.
Just like that astronaut.
Even if souls do lots of training,
like thousands of lives
before even coming on *this* trip.
They still go to sleep on the way.
And they forget.

But there's a reason for forgetting.
God did it on purpose.
If souls remembered
how good it was up in heaven,
they might decide to turn right around.
Some people feel that way anyway.
They really don't want to be here.
Like they're standing naked
at the edge of the ocean.
Dipping a toe into cold water.
And shivering.
Getting into that body is pretty hard.
And it's not so easy for the body either.
It doesn't all feel like love and light.
You've probably figured that out already.

I have a suspicion.
God wanted humans to be a little confused.

To think they *are* the body
right at the beginning.
Otherwise, too much information,
as the saying goes.
Souls get here on a need-to-know basis.
Like that baby duck
who woke up next to a mother hen.
Thought it must be a chicken.
The same way a soul wakes up in a body
and thinks it must be a body.
That thought can last a long time.

Did I mention the ghosts?
Every good story needs some ghosts.
What God is doing here is an experiment.
Even getting souls on the planet
and into those bodies.
There were some rough spots.
There were failures.
Prototypes that didn't quite work.
I'm sure God would admit it
if we were to ask.
Think about this.
When those astronauts took off for the moon,
some of them didn't get back.
That was an experiment that didn't work out.
There were plants and animals
the molecules couldn't quite get right.
Those aren't around anymore.

Were there souls that didn't make it into bodies?
And souls that didn't make it back?
Some got stuck in between heaven and earth.
Maybe since the beginning of human time.
And they've stayed there.
I wouldn't blame them
if they weren't happy about it.
I'm sure we can all understand that.

I've looked across death's threshold.
I've seen some very old souls.
Some of them are not very pleasant at all.
They are like a neighbor without any tools,
who wants to borrow yours.
Or steal them if you aren't looking.
Some of those souls reach into bodies
when bodies sleep
and souls dream of home.
Or when a body's soul isn't well attached.
And they've taken what they can.
They've done that for a long time.
You need to learn
how to protect your own energy,
or you might not like what is done with it.
I'm sure other people have seen the same as me.
We've felt them in our guts.
But don't mistake them for evil.
Nothing God has put into motion is evil.
Humans have had to create that.

Just the same,
you won't want to run into those souls.
Or even regular ghosts.
Like Uncle Al's soul.
That just got stuck
because it didn't know
to go to the light.
And because the churches forgot
how to get souls back across
when they become confused.

But try being less afraid
and a little softer.
Remember those souls started just like you.
You might not be here
if it weren't for them.
You might try remembering
with your heart.

You'll know who they really are.
No harm as long as you're careful.
Anchoring your soul in the heart
is protection enough.
I'm telling you about these ghosts for a reason.
They remind us of one very important thing.
What God started here isn't finished.
It's a process.
I think we've just gotten started.
Really.
History is not over.
Or Herstory either.

Well, back to *this* story.
God had to wake up those sleepy souls.
Souls needed to remember.
They came for a reason.
They needed to get to work.
So God left a hint.
Though we might think it was a dirty trick.
That hint is pain.
Pain can wake up anybody.
At least anybody
who really doesn't want to keep sleeping.
Some souls only need a little poke
to get on to remembering.
Like an itch
that just needs to be scratched.
But some souls need a lot more than an itch.
Either way, pain is the alarm clock.
We all need one
if we're not going to sleep this precious life away.
I bet your own mother told you that.

Pain eventually makes us think.
Like, what is going wrong here?
Nothing catches our attention like pain.
If a little doesn't work,
there's more where that came from.

Pain can pull your attention
to the most important thing in your life.
That would be *you*.
And who you are.
And why you came here in the first place.
Pain makes you focus.
At some point,
it makes you focus on what's not working.
On what might make you feel better.
Nothing makes us feel better
than being who we are.
There's nothing like it,
being who you are.
Not being you is the greatest pain.
Just try numbing out *that* pain.
You'll discover that it doesn't feel better.
It doesn't let you feel you at all.
But when you do what you came to do,
you'll feel something new.
I call it passion.
There's nothing like a life full of passion.
Passion is what we feel
when we let ourselves go
and just be who we are.
And nobody can do that for you.
Not some healer
or some guru.
You have to do it.
And there's some good news.
You don't have to do it all by yourself.
There's lots of help.
Light and sound are full of information.
You just have to tune in to the right channel.
That frequency is encoded right here,
on your own soul.
Which is why you have to pay attention.
In the heart.
And listen.

That's where we can feel that passion.
When you feel that passion,
you are on the trail of your destiny.
When you suffer with the pain,
I call that fate.
It's a good thing we have fate to wake us up.
Or we might never find our passion.
Polarity again.

Just enough discomfort in our lives
keeps us working at feeling better.
That's how we finally give up on thinking
that we can think our way out.
That's when we head for the heart.
Some of us won't try that heart out
until we get desperate.
I like to think of television as a gift.
Enough television
should make anybody desperate.
Sometimes we need a real loud wake-up call.
Ever hear someone say
the cancer was the best thing
that ever happened?
How could that be?
Well, it brought them
to what's really important.
It made them head for the heart.
And they found some answers there.
Standing at death's door gets your attention.

Almost dying is a great way
to figure out what's important.
There are many people
—you all know one—
who almost died.
Some came back with stories.
Stories about what they saw
and what they felt.
Stories about another side.

And one thing they saw,
they are not the body.
They were not the one
lying on the operating table.
Or the body lying next to a wrecked car.
They knew they were that other thing.
The soul.
Polarity.
Brought to you in high definition.

There's another way
to get the message.
There are magic plants.
Magic that opens doors in the brain.
When those doors get opened,
we see into mysteries.
We see into other universes
and deep into our own bodies.
We feel God's love
with nothing in between.
We feel the love of Earth
with nothing in between.
We know instantly.
We are not these little bodies.
And right there, we figure it out.
How to bring that big love
into these little bodies.
That's when we figure out the dance.
Polarity in motion.

All along, the heart has been waiting.
Here in the dark center of the body.
Just waiting
for someone to pay it some attention.
Just waiting
for someone to come home and turn it on.
Like that country-western singer said.
Just waiting
to open the door to the whole universe.

If someone would just take time to be curious.
The heart doesn't need any pain
or dying or plants.
It just needs the soul
to come home.
And to know who it is.
A soul curious enough to ask questions.
The heart provides the door
to all the answers you need.
It knows which direction the passion lies.
Just saying.
In case you want some passion in your life.

One more thing about that passion.
Don't make the mistake of thinking
you understand what it is.
You need to *know* what it is.
You can talk about God
and love and passion.
But talk's just talk.
Until you have tasted passion for yourself.
You can read a book
about climbing a mountain.
It might feel like you were there.
But you weren't.
If you really want to know,
you have to climb that mountain.
That's what I mean about tasting passion.
Get a taste.
It will change your life.

Well, myself, I was asleep.
Pretty numbed out.
I was pretty damn slow
in starting to listen.
God threw a near-death at me.
More than that.
God hit me in the head.
Knocked me down.

With one of those plants.
And when I came around,
I found myself in my heart.
Things have been different since.
I've felt a lot better.
And I'll say this.
Again.
There is nothing like passion.
After one taste,
there was no going back.

God created lots of ways
for humans to discover who they are.
God hid those ways in pain
and accidents and plants and the heart.
Some of us may have numbed too long.
That would be a sad story indeed.
But I think it's not your story.

Like I said,
there was a reason for hiding who you are,
like who you are is a secret.
Humans needed a lot of experience
just being on the planet.
They needed to figure out simple things,
like just surviving.
Then they could get on
with the more complicated things.
Like learning how to be themselves.
They needed some time to live life a little.
They needed to discover what doesn't work.
They needed some good ol' failures.
They needed to have a relationship or two,
and to fall on their faces.
Nothing like a relationship
to provide a little pain,
and let you know
you weren't paying attention.

Okay.
We're to that part of our story
where the soul is up and rubbing its eyes.
It's rolled over in bed
and discovered a strange body.
I bet you've had that experience.
Well.
The soul's got some work to do now.
It has to figure out how to get that body
to fall in love.
In love with the soul.

Now, here is the challenge.
We need to look at the body
and its pitiful personality
through the heart too.
They need all the compassion the soul can muster.
Remember.
It's the body that has suffered pain.
It's the body that experiences
a world that feels hostile.
It's the body that experiences fear.
Your body probably carries a lot of fear.
And a body in fear
doesn't trust anything or anybody.
Including a soul that is hovering around.
The soul needs to study up real fast.
Understanding polarity is a good place to start.
So, speaking to you souls out there
(the bodies can take a little nap here),
I want to say a little more about polarity.

Polarity is just like attraction.
Like when you see that man or woman
who really catches your attention.
It's like two magnets racing toward each other.
We've all felt that.
We say opposites attract.
That's how magnets are.

Some people like to call that polarity
by the name of duality.
As though everything but God itself
is this duality.
Some people like to say
that duality is illusion.
They say that only God
(or unity or love—one of those names)
is real.
Well.
I would say that everything God has a hand in *is* God.
Left hand *or* right hand.
And that is everything.
It's all real,
including the polarity or duality or opposites.
Whatever you want to call it.
Nothing is not real.
Even if there are lots of differences
in those realities.
But isn't that the whole point of creation?

All polarities have a very special quality.
That would be *com-ple-men-tar-ity.*
Complementarity means that the parts
have a special connection.
A connection that is about potential.
Take soul and body.
Soul and body are a polarity.
They have a special potential,
A potential that can't happen
unless the body lets the soul in.
Until the soul and the body
can figure out how to work
with each other.
Until they can resonate together.
Until they can collaborate.
The connection they start with
is only a connection.
The soul has to turn that connection

into a collaboration,
into a relationship
that empowers that complementarity.
A collaboration that can create something
never created before.
That's why we're here.
To figure out what our complementarity is.
So we can discover what we came to create.

I say God has created humans
to create something out of matter.
To create something
out of density.
Out of the slowest of frequencies.
If God was going to create something,
there had to be a way to do it.
And humans are the way God chose.
At least on this planet.

Humans are not only in a process.
They are the process.
You are a process.
There might have been other ways.
But here on planet blue,
that's what God decided to do.
God put freedom into humans.
And a way to learn how to use it.
Even God doesn't know
what that might create.
That is the fun part.
It wouldn't be very interesting otherwise.
Even to God.

So humans are engines of creation.
And souls are the part that God whispers into.
And hearts are the ears that souls listen with.
Bodies are the part that souls whisper into.
If the soul wants to create,
it needs a body that feels safe.

Safe enough to connect.
Safe enough to let its life force flow.
The heart knows where to go,
and mind can plan the trip.
Passion puts pedal to the metal.
And love lets matter's life force
rise up like sap in the body,
with power enough to break concrete
and build whatever the soul might imagine.
And what did that woman sing?
Love is just another word
for nothing left to lose.
What are you waiting for?
What do you have to lose?

Back to the story.
We left off
where the soul woke up
and found a strange body in bed.
Right there and then,
the soul knows it has work to do.
Like I said,
the soul has to get that body to fall in love.
With the soul.
Because the body won't let that soul in
unless it feels safe and loved.
Just like a wise woman.
A woman who won't let a man in,
really in,
unless she feels safe and loved.
Particularly if they've wound up in bed.

That brings me to one important thing
I don't want to forget.
There's a lot of talk
about the masculine and the feminine.
And about that patriarchy.
Anybody who can understand anything
knows that patriarchy isn't a good thing.

Men haven't accounted for themselves
at all well.
Those women who said it were right.
Men just don't get it, most of them.
Those men push corporations around
like toy trucks.
Running over toy governments
and the rest of us too.
So some say that we need to stop all that.
Some say we need a matriarchy.
But I say
women who are equal to men
can be equally good patriarchs.
What we need is balance.
And that is not a statistic.
Equality isn't balance, even if it's a start.
It's about polarity and complementarity.

I know men have tortured women.
Those men torture their own souls the same.
There are a few women who have done the same.
We throw those words *masculine* and *feminine*
like stones.
I say, make them into pathways.
Walk them in the direction of experience.
That's the direction of truth, yours and mine.
Go inside where words don't matter.
Don't try to tell me.
Show me what you find there.

I say men and women are differently the same.
In each of us,
there is capacity for action and for non-action.
There is a capacity for giving and for receiving.
All of us have the ability
to penetrate and to be penetrated.
All of us can contain and contribute.
All of us have a mind
that breaks things into parts

and a heart that connects.
We all have feelings.
We all bleed when we are cut.
Just because you are a man
doesn't tell us what kind of person you are.
Or what kind of person you could be.
The same for women.
Tell me a person's gender
and I still know almost nothing about them.
God made many genders.
And any woman can betray a man
with the same lie that a man can tell.
Gender is just one form
of ten thousand trillion polarities.
All dancing.
All the time.

In your dance, the lead keeps shifting.
Do you know who is leading?
Earth's poles are shifting.
The sun's fields are shifting.
Do you think yours are doing less?
Everything is moving now.
Changes are coming fast.
They will not wait
for your small mind to catch up.
Pretending it can run the show.

What I want to know is this.
Have you walked into the pain?
Have you tasted fierceness in your soul?
And wildness in your body?
Do you know how to love?
And how not to strike out
in fear and violent anger?
We'll all feel that.
Can you find your truth?
Can you express that truth
in gentle actions and soft words?

Can you connect?
And connect without judgment and projection?
Can you be hard when you need to be
and soft when you don't?
And can you just be?
And be in the truth of who you are?
Can you get body and soul together?
And get on with the work of creation?
Do you know where your passion lies?
Have you thrown your small self
into the turbulent center of that passion?
Have you opened small mind to earth's soul
and sky's infinity?
Can you sniff the cosmic wind?
Have you cast heart's net into the cosmic ocean?
And what shining, wriggling knowing have you caught?

Thinking God is a man doesn't serve anything.
You can't touch God with mere thinking.
Believe in belief if you like,
but even churches can't sell it anymore.
Experience God
and your belief might mean something.
At least to you.
You won't need that church at all.
Or that guru either.
Let scientists study gender.
Let scientists believe that evolution
invented kindness to diminish fear.
I'll experience my own heart
and be the soul.
I'll study what the heart sees,
and kiss my own feet,
thank you very much.

We don't need to argue whether earth is a woman
or heaven a man.
Every thing is made of polarities.
Not of contradictions,

but complementarities.
Earth is mother to our childish play.
That mother may await our growing up
for another moment or two.
But not much longer.
How would you feel mothering teenagers?
Teenagers intoxicated with sleep,
wrecking the family car.
Earth may be as soft as a breast,
but can be hard as any man.
And can love more than you know.
We are about to find out about earth's rage.
Tell me.
Is that feminine or masculine?
And what does it matter?

So what is God's left hand?
It is this.
This earth.
That man.
That woman.
And all genders in between.
And heat and cold.
Light *and* dark.
Whatever little that is awake
and the more that isn't.
Soul complements body.
Just like body complements soul.
Heaven complements this earth.
What is the right foot without the left?

I know this much.
We are God's left hand.
With animals and plants and rocks.
With all of earth and water and air and fire.
With light and sound.
And with all of earth's spirits
and little beings you've never seen.
They see you.

And with dogs and cats and horses.
Whose hearts were sent to teach you love.
And plants that feed and heal.
And let you see beyond your little self.
Evil?
What you would call evil
is the random acts of a human whose soul is asleep.
A body pulsing with life's formidable force.
A body driven
by the fear of being alone.
Alone while its soul sleeps.
There is nothing so wasted or reckless
as a body without its soul mate.
That mate would be you,
when you know yourself to be the soul.
When that body falls in love,
what you would call evil will be no more.
Do not try to tame the body.
No need.
Just don't confuse it with the soul.
Just taste it,
and don't let it control you.
Wildness is its nature.
You will need that.
Wildness is life force itself.
Love it.
Embrace it.
Invite it to the dance.
God created that body to dance with you.

And feel that body's pain.
Run into it.
As fast as you can.
Embrace it too.
Kiss it.
Welcome it.
Thank it for coming.
If it hit you hard, thank it twice.
Say, I needed that.

Say, thank you so very much.
Say, if I fall asleep, hit me again.
Unwrap the pain and find your gift.
That's where you'll find the soul snoozing.
Your growing awareness is pain's gift.
Know your growing attention
your growing focus
as soul gathering itself.
Gathering for the journey.
No more.
No less.
Be that soul.
Gather yourself in the center of the heart.
And rivet yourself to *that* center.
To that fulcrum.
To that portal.
And explode your radiance into the universe.

You know the heart of which I speak.
Not the pulsing part
or even that celebrity chakra.
I speak of the heart *field*.
The one that stretches beyond creation.
The field that connects
the tiny soul to every thing.
And what's behind things.
The field that penetrates the mystery.
Let the soul race into that.
Let mind tag along.
Then emotions and thoughts
will settle themselves.
Then body can bathe
in that glittering pool.
And feel safe and loved.
Then the body will fall in love with you.
You!
The soul your body was made for.

This is how the left hand works.
Don't take my word for it.
Just dive in.
Then I'll listen to your words.
I'll listen to anyone
who journeys out of time.
I'll listen to any soul
standing in the heart.
My mind may not understand.
But I'll know
which direction your words point.
And I'll say thank you.
Thank you.
Sing that song again.
I like to listen to *that* music.
And I'll dance to my own.

Some say
the left hand is the side of darkness.
I say, race into that darkness.
Some say
the right hand is the side of God.
I say
God has two hands.
Some want to sit at God's right hand.
I say *you* are God's left hand.
And that you are sitting
exactly where you need to be.

AUTHOR'S AFTERWORD

IN MY FIRST BOOK, *The Soul's Critical Path,* I used thousands of words to describe the difference between fate and destiny and how these forces provide the background for the soul's planetary journey of embodiment and creation. With prose, I could flesh out a point of view—my personal experience translated into an understanding. Prose uses the tool of analysis and its assistants: logic, definitions, distinctions, illustrations, graphs, and a few stories to break the monotony.

If prose labors all day to present a respectable understanding, poetry takes only a moment to share a knowing. If I had used poetry to describe the difference between fate and destiny, I could have just said that fate is lemons, and destiny is lemonade. If you have ever created something beautiful out of a challenge, you would instantly know what I mean. More words would not have added much to the effective communication of that simple observation.

We use prose to create a construct, which is a mental perspective. "Understanding" is the word I use to describe that perspective, although the word is often used to describe something more for which I reserve the term "knowing." By knowing, I mean a different way of seeing that arises in the heart. Mental constructs are never complete, or completely accurate, ways to describe anything of any complexity, and all "things" have a degree of complexity humans have not unraveled. To paraphrase a British author whose name I can't recall, once you get past saying "pass the gravy," language loses its capacity to convey truth directly.

Nevertheless, we continue to press prose into such service, and we do so at length, perhaps hoping that length will compensate for absent essence. Our increasingly scientific culture demands that we process our speculations with its methodology, a specialized form of understandings marketed as "objective" and "research based," neither of which is as true as we would like to believe. Our embrace of scientific method, for all its benefits and potential, includes a jealous streak. That voice shames the subjective and personal, and attempts to strip simple heart-based knowings out of those presumably superior understandings. This impoverished science has abandoned an epistemology of direct knowing based in personal experience. That abandonment is a dangerous trend against which poetry persists as it struggles to find a booth in the epistemological marketplace. Greater scientists, such as Einstein, acknowledged his knowings as a foundational aspect of his process of creating brilliant, if incomplete, understandings. Not all science is devoid of the subjective heart.

Poetry embraces the subjective. In so doing, it embraces heart as an epistemological source that mere mental process cannot touch. Poetry aims not at communicating an understanding, but at a momentary fellowship, a moment of connection between two people who might share respective personal experiences that have given rise to the same knowing.

A knowing is instantaneous, *felt* before it might be reduced to a thought. We know with our hearts. "'Do you love your dog?' he said. 'Of course,' she said, without hesitating for the time it might take to inventory the dog's virtues. She simply knew. Nothing to explain. No rational defense necessary. He lived with a dog himself, though the nature of her animal—its erratic peeing and moldy rug odor—made it difficult to understand how anyone could love hers. But his own dog would win no award either, at least none other than his own heart. So he knew what she meant, while his mind could only concede the possibility that love might extend that far."

That is the nature of knowing. It is immediate, and it is completely personal, at the same time it touches universal experience. Understandings, as I use the term, are not instantaneous, are less personal, and are further removed from the experience that gives rise to a knowing.

But even poetry isn't all-knowing. Whatever speaks to the poet from the other side inevitably touches the personality on the way through to the poet's mental field, itself subject to the limitations of language. The personality and its cherished but inherently flawed understandings are formidable filters to the information that flows from fields of intelligence that lie beyond this dimension. These fields inform our intuitions, insights, visions, knowings, and, ultimately, our poetry.

It requires deep listening to tune our heart-receivers beyond the personality's static, which is why poems that do come to me come during a heart-centric form of meditation—a process by which I have gradually learned to listen with the soul's ear. As we have all heard, the soul does not sit in the mind. It finds its home away from home in what we often call the "heart"—even though we have little understanding of what that word might mean once we get past the pumping part.

Still, I've learned to place my attention in the chest, where the mythic heart is rumored to live, because the quality of information I get in that place is beyond what the mind produces, even if the mind may process that information into useful and beautiful understandings. I say "useful," because any notion of complete understandings, if that phrase were to imply an ultimate truth, is an oxymoron. Understandings are never complete, because they are at best a process of grounding an ever-changing landscape of experience into just enough constants to let us navigate. I say thanks to science for chasing after those constants, but I suspect we will find them more directly in a collaboration between personal experience and scientific investigations.

I tried to explain this notion of heart-listening to an inventor friend who is an electrical engineer. I thought he came up with a good understanding of this heart-knowing process. He said he had been able to propagate low frequency signals through the earth and hear them at a distance by using the Fourier transform and reducing the bandwidth almost to zero. I sensed that I have to get my own soul-ear to listen so finely that a zero bandwidth is a pretty good description for it. But try teaching a meditation class with that understanding.

When I get a clear jingle from beyond the personality, I race to my computer with the magic phrase that has come through. I write those words down and listen for more. If there are more, the entire poem appears almost immediately. My personal input seems more like recorder than author. I don't write those poems so much as lay them out and try to smooth the wrinkles that too much time in the personality's dryer has created. When a poem becomes hard work, I just stop, hit delete, and wait for another day.

The poems that stay are personal in another way. If there is any wisdom in a poem, I try to remember that it came not from me, but *for* me—carrying some perspective that I needed to integrate into my own life. Consequently, I have found that my understandings of these poems evolve over the years or find affirmation in experiences that arrive long after the poem itself.

The central theme of these poems reflects the central theme in my life, which is a passion for exploring that aspect of consciousness humans have long called the soul, and how soul accesses life force through the body and earth to form a partnership in service of creation. So it is not surprising to me that these poems have arrived as any other peak spiritual experience, with all the joy and fresh physical sense of a light-wave passing through the body. Like other spiritual experiences, a poem requires a process of integration that comes from a continuing presence to the gifts the experience brings. So I find myself rereading my poems from time to time to mine any guidance I have missed.

Many of these poems have arisen in the context of personal relationships. I often thought a particular poem was for the woman with whom I was in relationship at the time. In retrospect, I sense that those relationships graciously provided the emotional openings that created a path for other-dimensional messages to reach my heart, having failed to penetrate my prosaic mind.

Those openings allowed messages of guidance to push past the conflicted personality's common domination of consciousness. In our culture, that domination has a particularly mental flavor. The heart becomes available at the behest of its first cousin, the emotions. I say emotions and heart are first cousins because we read them both with a feeling sense. But they are not the same thing, as is often surmised. The mind's thoughts, on the other hand, seem to belong to another tribe altogether.

That suggests to me one important reason that relationships provide a primary context for spiritual evolution. Relationships force emotions out of hiding and into the open where we can see them, allowing us to work with the hidden information that they carry. Emotions are the doorway to the unconsciously held defense patterns that form in the body in response to trauma. The body's memory of its traumas has far more control over our behaviors than the mind's beliefs, despite the mind's arrogant assumption that it is independent of our feelings. The underbelly of most of our unexamined thinking is an unacknowledged feeling.

Apart from my relationship with my partner Darlene, who shares the dedication of this book with my first and best childhood friend Janie, one of those relationships continues in real time. *Green Eyed Lover* speaks of my relationship with a cosmic-level field of intelligence. That relationship was initially hosted by the Amazonian plant medicine *ayahuasca,* which is also known as the vine of the soul. It has the capacity to push the personality aside almost completely for a short time, during which physical healing and some very direct interdimensional communication can occur. My accounts of those encounters can be found in my books *The Soul's Critical Path* and *Soul Tribes and Tambos.*

The language of these poems also reflects an ongoing fusion of my practice of various forms of meditation with my experience of indigenous shamanism. *Where Are the Old Ones?* refers to the *chakaruna*, a word found in the indigenous Quechua language that still thrives in much of South America. It means "human bridge"—referring to a person who crosses back and forth from our familiar three-dimensional world to other dimensions in order to communicate with fields of intelligence that reside there. Souls that become self-aware and learn to focus their attention can become such bridges. Those bridge-souls work in service to the evolution of other souls and the evolution of consciousness in general.

Such soul work inevitably connects us with the dying process. The last poem in Part One of this collection, *Beauty Turns My Head*, arrived as I was searching for a simple way of speaking to a friend with whom I sat while he died of pancreatic cancer. I ultimately saw the poem as a way to talk to myself about death, since I felt that it was not my role as his caretaker to push my own understandings at him.

So my poetry represents an important part of the soul's process of coming into self-awareness. Most of these poems were written while I was slowly awakening to my identity as soul, and each poem represents a landmark on that journey. This shift of identity has given rise to a new way of looking at my experience—what I have called in my other books a *soul perspective.*

A soul perspective is not simply a concept or a belief, but a lived, experiential identification with soul. That identification can hold the body, mind, emotions, and personality at enough distance to permit the emerged soul to see itself as an entity distinct from those other aspects of humans. With that distance, the soul can discover its own impulses and imperatives. It can see fate as a process distinct from the process of personal destiny. While we suffer fate, we can create destiny by walking into fate's challenges armed with the soul's own strengths. From that perspective, the soul can recognize the body as its first and most significant soul mate. When the soul can bring the sense of love and safety to the body that is the condition for the body to fall in love with the soul, the soul will have gained the strong legs it needs to do its work of creation on the planet.

In Part Two, which is a single piece entitled *The Left Hand of God*, I have shifted to the middle ground between poetry and prose sometimes called prose poetry. It contains elements of poetry, but forms more of a story than a prose exposition. I have abandoned the accepted form of punctuation that prose demands. Instead, I have used punctuation that mimics a spoken, colloquial style in which a story might be told. I did not intend that style. It is just how it came out, and I did my best to convey the style of what I heard. I like it best when it is read out loud. Thanks to my proofreader Elisabeth Hallett for working with this nonconforming style.

Stories are themselves a middle ground. The mind cannot penetrate the ultimate mysteries of creation, and the heart cannot articulate what it knows without mind. So humans have resorted to story as the most effective way of communicating both our experience and received knowledge of those mysteries. While stories speak of truth, they cannot tell the truth. So we need not believe them to reap their value. That value comes when we listen carefully to the feelings and knowings that stories evoke in our own hearts.

A story's real value is to lead us away from mind's limitations long enough to enter into an experiential encounter with the mystery that is wholly, or holy, personal. Only a deep personal knowing will truly allow us to navigate the mystery. Consequently, the best stories are the ones that call us from the impersonal to the personal—from mere understandings to inherently personal knowings, from which our respective minds can re-form understandings of their own.

When the story points to an overarching mystery that is universally relevant to human experience, we may call the story-understanding a *myth*. The origin stories from many cultures are each such a myth. When the theory of evolution purports to explain creation, it becomes myth despite being told in scientific language. It's not at all clear that the scientific story has surpassed the origin myths of various cultures in clearing up the mystery.

Sometimes the storyteller wants you to believe the story is true so you will buy the story and support the teller instead of heading for the mystery on your own. We call that kind of storytelling by the name "religion." Even science includes a bit of that kind of storytelling.

So we would all do well to take care not to fall into the trap of thinking those stories—prose, poetry, or scientific—are more than mere pointers, more true than what we can know in our hearts, or more valuable than direct, personal experience.

And that challenge is as old as Eden.

ABOUT THE AUTHOR

John P. Davidson writes and teaches about the evolution of the soul. He lives in the United States and travels to Peru. He may be contacted at www.soulscriticalpath.com

www.ingramcontent.com/pod-product-compliance
Lightning Source LLC
Chambersburg PA
CBHW051814040426
42446CB00007B/670